My State WASHINGTON

By Christina Earley

TABLE OF CONTENTS

Washington 3

Glossary 22

Index 24

A Crabtree Seedlings Book

Crabtree Publishing

crabtreebooks.com

School-to-Home Support for Caregivers and Teachers

This book helps children grow by letting them practice reading. Here are a few guiding questions to help the reader build his or her comprehension skills. Possible answers appear in red.

Before Reading:

- What do I know about Washington?
    - *I know that Washington is a state.*
    - *I know that Washington has mountains.*
- What do I want to learn about Washington?
    - *I want to learn which famous people were born in Washington.*
    - *I want to learn what the state flag looks like.*

During Reading:

- What have I learned so far?
    - *I have learned that Olympia is the state capital of Washington.*
    - *I have learned that Washington grows the most apples in the U.S.*
- I wonder why...
    - *I wonder why the state flower is the Pacific rhododendron.*
    - *I wonder why there are glaciers in Olympic National Park.*

After Reading:

- What did I learn about Washington?
    - *I have learned that the Space Needle is 605 feet (184 m) tall.*
    - *I have learned that the state animal is the Olympic marmot.*
- Read the book again and look for the glossary words.
    - *I see the word* ***lavender*** *on page 5, and the word* ***capital*** *on page 6. The other glossary words are found on pages 22 and 23.*

WASHINGTON
Hi! My name is Haruki. Welcome to Washington!

I live in Sequim. My city is next to the Dungeness River.

Sequim is known for its beautiful **lavender** fields.

Washington is in the northwestern United States. The **capital** is Olympia.

Fun Fact: Seattle is the largest city in Washington.

The state animal is the Olympic marmot.

The Pacific rhododendron is the state flower.

We grow a lot of apples in Washington. Some of them are used to make apple pie.

Fun Fact: Washington grows the most apples in the U.S.

My state flag is green. The state **seal** is in the middle.

My family and I like to watch the Seattle Seahawks play football.

Olympic National Park has many different areas to explore. My favorite is the Hoh **Rain Forest** because it feels like a jungle.

Fun Fact: There are around 200 **glaciers** in Olympic National Park.

I enjoy swimming with my family in Lake Chelan.

I like to visit the Space Needle in Seattle. It's a tower that's 605 feet (184 m) tall!

Bill Gates, the **cofounder** of Microsoft, was born in Washington. Actress Dove Cameron was also born in Washington.

Fun Fact: Patty Murray, the first woman from Washington to be elected to the U.S. Senate, was born in Bothell, Washington.

I like going on picnics at Snoqualmie Falls.

I love to go to Mount Rainier National Park in the summer and take pictures of all the beautiful flowers.

Glossary

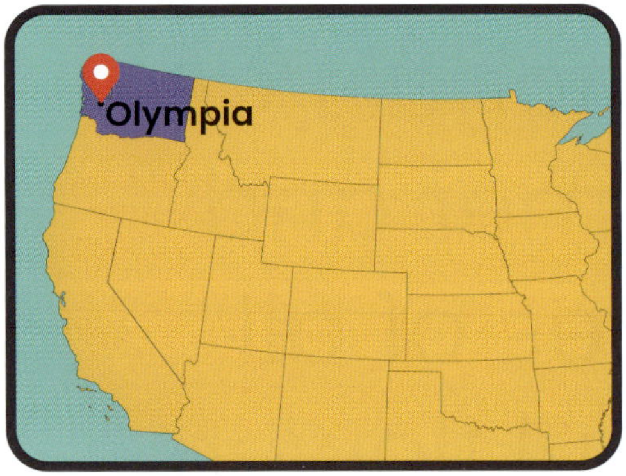

capital (cap-ih-tuhl): The city or town where the government of a country, state, or province is located

cofounder (koh-foun-der): A person who starts a business with other people

glacier (glay-sher): A large body of ice and snow that moves slowly over a large area of land

lavender (lav-ihn-der): A plant with small purple flowers that have a sweet smell

rain forest (rayn for-ist): A forest that receives a lot of rain and that has very tall trees

seal (seel): A special design that is used on important papers and other items

Index

apples 10, 11
Gates, Bill 18
lavender 5
Olympia 6
Olympic National Park 14
swimming 16

About the Author

Christina Earley lives in sunny South Florida with her husband and son. She enjoys traveling around the United States and learning about different historical places. Her hobbies include hiking, yoga, and baking.

Written by: Christina Earley
Designed and Illustrated by: Bobbie Houser
Series Development: James Earley
Proofreader: Melissa Boyce
Educational Consultant: Marie Lemke M.Ed.

Photographs:
Alamy: ZUMA Press, Inc.: p. 19
Newscom: Sven Hoppe/dpa/picture-alliance: p. 13
Shutterstock: Jeff McGraw: cover; David B. Petersen: p. 3; Jnjphotos: p. 4; blueeyes: p. 5, 23; Volina: p. 6, 22; Sean Pavone: p. 7, 20; Virginie Merckaert: p. 8; Julian Popov: p. 9; jewelspics: p. 10-11; 5 second Studio: p. 11; Creative Photo Corner: p. 12, 23; Tobin Akehurst: p. 14, 22; f11photo: p. 14-15, 23; Frank L Junior: p. 16; cpaulfell: p. 17; Frederic Legrand - COMEO: p. 18 left, 22; Quinn Jeffrey: p. 18 right; Roman Khomlyak: p. 21

Crabtree Publishing

crabtreebooks.com 800-387-7650

Printed in the U.S.A./072023/CG20230214

Published in Canada
Crabtree Publishing
616 Welland Avenue
St. Catharines, Ontario
L2M 5V6

Published in the United States
Crabtree Publishing
347 Fifth Avenue
Suite 1402-145
New York, New York, 10016

Library and Archives Canada Cataloguing in Publication
Available at Library and Archives Canada

Library of Congress Cataloging-in-Publication Data
Available at the Library of Congress

Hardcover: 978-1-0398-0540-8
Paperback: 978-1-0398-0572-9
Ebook (pdf): 978-1-0398-0636-8
Epub: 978-1-0398-0604-7